DANGERS OF THE DEEP

Contents

The Case of the Lake Monster — page 2

Monsters of the Deep — page 18

Simon Cheshire

Story illustrated by
Ned Woodman

Before Reading

In this story

 Harry

 Kate

 Mr Stone

Tricky words

- hotel
- thought
- bleating
- dreaming
- footprint
- faint

 Introduce these tricky words and help the reader when they come across them later!

Story starter

Harry and Kate are members of SCARY, a secret club that investigates spooky mysteries. One day, they heard about mysterious happenings in a lake near a hotel – a monster was reported to have been killing sheep.

The Case of the Lake Monster

Harry and Kate went to the hotel.

They met the hotel owner, Mr Stone.

"Tell us about the monster in the lake," said Harry.

"We want to find out what is really happening," said Kate.

"I haven't seen the monster myself," said Mr Stone. "But the farmers say it has killed five of their sheep. Lots of people in my hotel have come here to see it."

"I hope we get to see the monster," said Harry.

"If there *is* a monster," said Kate.

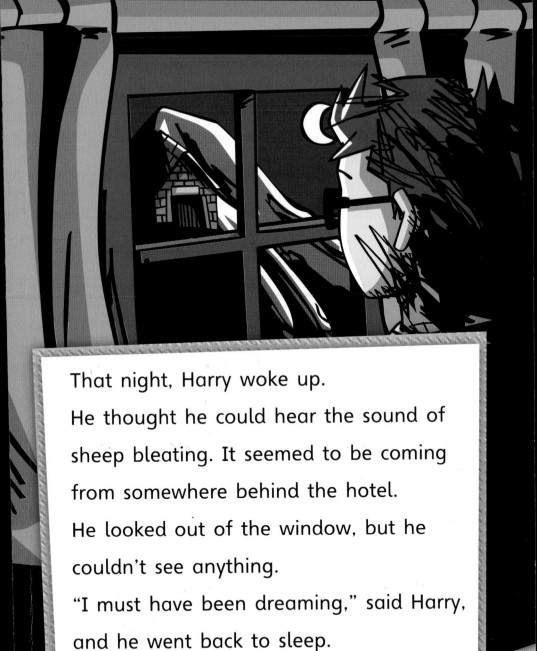

That night, Harry woke up.

He thought he could hear the sound of sheep bleating. It seemed to be coming from somewhere behind the hotel.

He looked out of the window, but he couldn't see anything.

"I must have been dreaming," said Harry, and he went back to sleep.

The next morning, Harry and Kate went to look at the lake. Lots of other hotel guests were also by the lake, looking for the monster. Harry and Kate met a farmer. He told them that the lake monster had struck again in the night.

"The monster has eaten another of my sheep," he said.

"Why do you think it was eaten by a monster?" said Kate.

The farmer pointed to some bits of fleece in the mud. Beside them were some marks – something had been dragged into the water!

Then Harry saw something else in the mud. "Look!" he cried. "It's a footprint – a huge footprint! That's proof that there's a monster."

"Just because there's a huge footprint doesn't mean there has to be a monster," said Kate. "Let's find out what made this footprint."

Harry and Kate went back to the hotel.
They searched the Internet for footprints
to match the one they had seen by
the lake.

"The footprint doesn't match any animal
here," said Kate.

"So it must belong to a monster in the
lake," said Harry.

"Or," said Kate, "the footprint, the bits of fleece and those drag marks were all put there to fool people."

"Well, if there's no monster," said Harry, "where did the missing sheep go?"

"That's what we have to find out!" said Kate.

Then Harry remembered that he had heard the faint sound of sheep bleating in the night. Perhaps he hadn't been dreaming after all! Could he have heard the missing sheep?

"Kate, I think I've worked it out!" cried Harry. "Come on!"

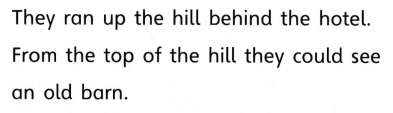

They ran up the hill behind the hotel.
From the top of the hill they could see
an old barn.
Then they heard the sound of sheep
bleating. They looked through a crack
in the barn door. Inside were six sheep.
"They must be the missing sheep,"
said Harry.

12

"Of course!" cried Kate. "Mr Stone wanted people to believe there was a monster in the lake. That way, he would always have lots of hotel guests."

"He must have made the drag marks and the huge footprint too," said Harry.

As they walked back to the hotel,
Harry looked down at the lake.

"Kate!" he cried. "Look at the lake!
I just saw a huge dark shape moving
in the water."

Kate looked at the lake.

"I can't see anything," she said.

"Well I saw *something* – I know I did!"
said Harry.

KATE'S REPORT

Mr Stone made up the story about the lake monster.

He knew that if people thought there was a monster, they would come and stay at his hotel.

I think all lake monsters are a myth!

HARRY'S REPORT

Mr Stone made the footprints near the lake and he hid the sheep in the barn.

But I know I saw something moving in the lake.

I think there are monsters in some lakes.

Quiz

Text Detective

- Why did Mr Stone want people to believe there was a monster in the lake?
- Whose report do you think is closest to the truth?

Word Detective

- **Phonic Focus**: Unstressed vowels
  Page 3: Which letters represent the unstressed vowel in 'owner' and 'monster'? (er)
- Page 8: Which adjective describes the footprint?
- Page 9: Which letter does the apostrophe replace in the word 'doesn't'?

Super Speller

Read these words:

anything   morning   thought

Now try to spell them!

HA! HA! HA!

Q Why is the letter 'V' like a monster?

A It comes after 'U'.

Find out about

- Reports of monsters said to live in the seas and lakes around the world

Tricky words

- evil
- metres
- proof
- fakes
- teenagers
- scales

Introduce these tricky words and help the reader when they come across them later!

Text starter

All over the world, there have been reports of monsters living in deep lakes or in the sea. Some monsters have long necks, some have green scales, and some even have horns! But are these monsters real or fake?

Monsters of the Deep

All over the world, there are lots of reports of monsters that live in the sea or in very deep lakes. There are even photos of some of these monsters!

But are there really 'monsters of the deep'?

A Cornish Monster

One day, two women were walking by the sea in Cornwall. They said that a huge monster came up out of the sea. It had a long neck and evil eyes. Then it dived down under the sea and came back up with a huge eel in its mouth!

A few years later, two men said they saw a monster coming up out of the sea. It was about five metres long. It had a small ugly head, and horns!
Later, some photos were found. They seemed to be of the sea monster.
But who took them and when were they taken?

Was this the monster the men saw?

A Scottish Monster

There is a very deep lake in Scotland called Loch Ness. A monster is said to live at the bottom of the lake. There have been many reports of this monster. People say that it is huge and it has a long neck and a long tail.

People call the monster Nessie.
Many people have taken photos of
strange shapes in the lake. They say that
these shapes are the monster and they
are proof that Nessie lives in the lake.
Some of these photos are fakes,
but others may not be.

The photo above is a fake, but the one to the left may be real.

A Canadian Monster

There is a very deep lake in Canada. A monster called Ogopogo is said to live in it. There have been many reports of this monster. People say that it is 20 metres long, with a thin body, and a long head which looks a bit like a snake.

In 1968, five teenagers were in a boat on the lake. They said they saw a huge dark shape in the water just below their boat. They said they could see green and grey scales. Could they have seen Ogopogo?

An American Monster

There is a very deep lake in America called Lake Champlain. A monster is said to live in the lake.

The man who first saw the monster said it was five metres long, with a head like a horse.

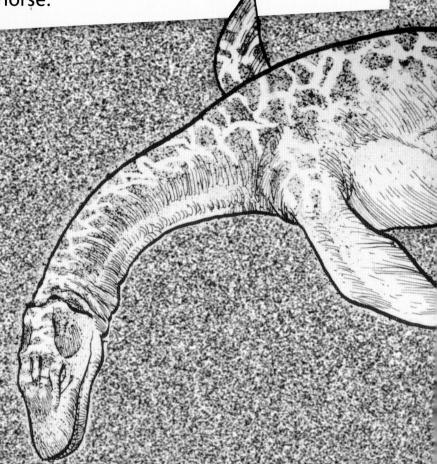

One day, two men were in a boat on the lake. They said they saw a huge dark monster. One of the men hit the monster with an oar and it dived down to the bottom of the lake!

They nicknamed the monster 'Champ'.

That same year, people on a ship saw a strange head rise out of the lake. Was it Champ looking at them?

A Russian Monster

There is a very deep lake in Russia.

In 1968, a scientist was by the lake.

Suddenly, a strange creature came up

out of the water. The monster had a long

neck, a dark body, and a fin along its back.

The scientist ran back to his friends and told them what he had seen. They did not believe him.

Then, later that day, some other scientists were by the lake. Suddenly, a huge monster rose up out of the lake. Was it the lake monster coming to get them?

A Swedish Monster

There is also said to be a monster in a big lake in Sweden.

In 1976, two men in a boat saw the monster swim around their boat. When they went back to the shore, the monster swam behind the boat all the way!

Why are there so many reports of monsters living in deep lakes or the sea? Is it because the lakes and seas are so deep that no one has ever been to the bottom? Or is it because there really are monsters down there?

What do you think?

Quiz

Text Detective

- What do people call the Loch Ness Monster?
- Which monster do you find most scary?

Word Detective

- **Phonic Focus:** Unstressed vowels
  Page 28: Which letters represent the unstressed vowel in 'creature'? (ure)
- Page 21: What different types of punctuation are used to end the sentences?
- Page 23: Find a word that means 'odd'.

Super Speller

Read these words:

head   suddenly   someone

Now try to spell them!

Q What do you call a lost monster?

A A where wolf!